First Edition
Genuine Autographed Collectible

Do you want me to sign it in ink or in lipstick?

World Famous Poems

The Greatest Poems Ever Written on Extraordinary World Events

Gift Card

Date:

To:

From:

Message:

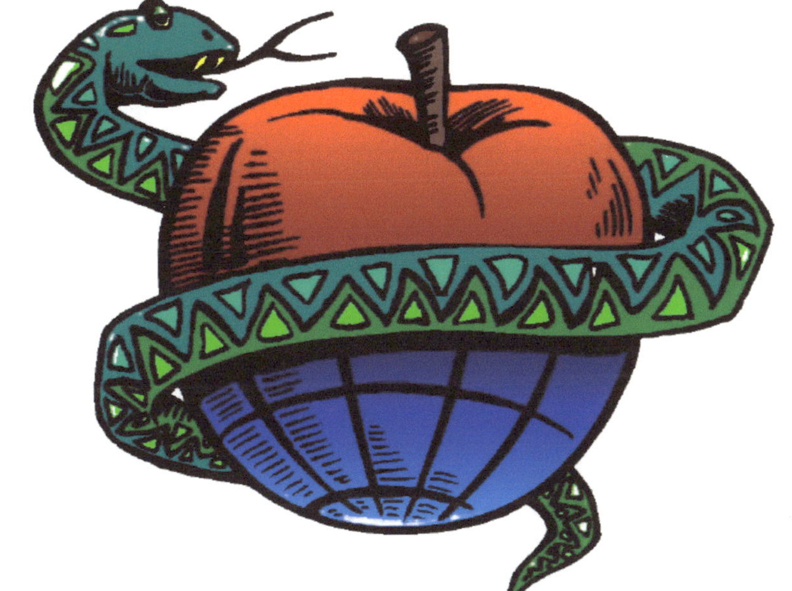

Literature, Poetry, Religion, Theology, Bible, Sharon Esther Lampert

Through the Eyes of Eve: POETRY WORLD RECORD

KADIMAH PRESS
GIFTS OF GENIUS

Books may be purchased for education, business, or sales promotional use.
ISBN Hardcover: 979-8-3485-2454-8
ISBN Paperback: 979-8-3485-2454-8
ISBN e-book: 979-8-3485-2457-9
Library of Congress Catalog Card Number: 2025904180

FAN MAIL:
SharonEstherLampert.com
FANS@SharonEstherLampert.com

Cover and Interior Book Design: Creative Genius Sharon Esther Lampert
Editor: Dave Segal

Palm Beach Book Publisher, Phone: 561-888-0313
Sharon@PalmBeachBookPublisher.com
To Order Book:
Ingram, 1 Ingram Blvd. La Vergne, TN 37086-3629
Phone: 615-793-5000
Fax orders: 615-287-6990

First Edition

Manufactured in the United States of America

World Famous Poem

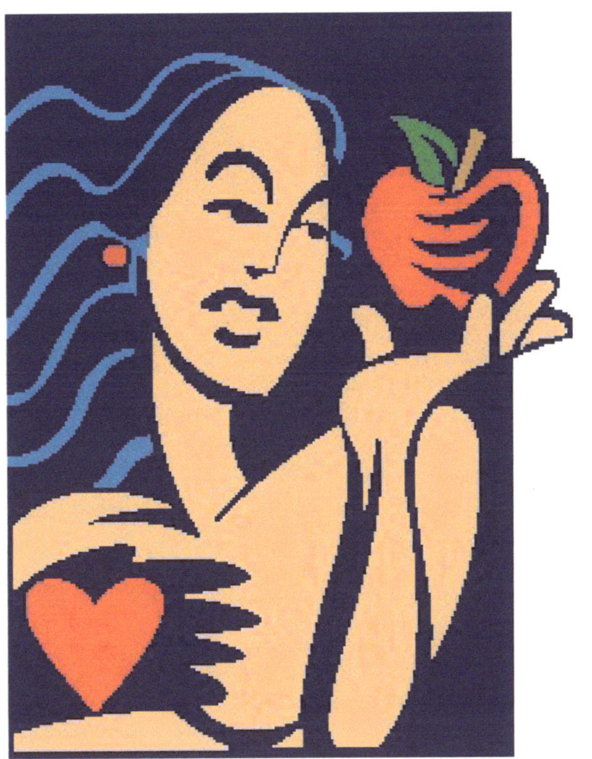

Through the Eyes of Eve

POETRY WORLD RECORD

120 Words of Rhyme From One Family of Rhyme

Sharon Esther Lampert

BE ART

ART IS SMART

ART IS FROM THE HEART

MAKE ART NOT WAR

YOU ARE BORN FOR GREATNESS

YOU ARE A MASTERPIECE

Sharon Esther Lampert

DEDICATION
MOMMY
LOVE OF MY LIFETIME
Who Knew Who I Was From the INSIDE OUT

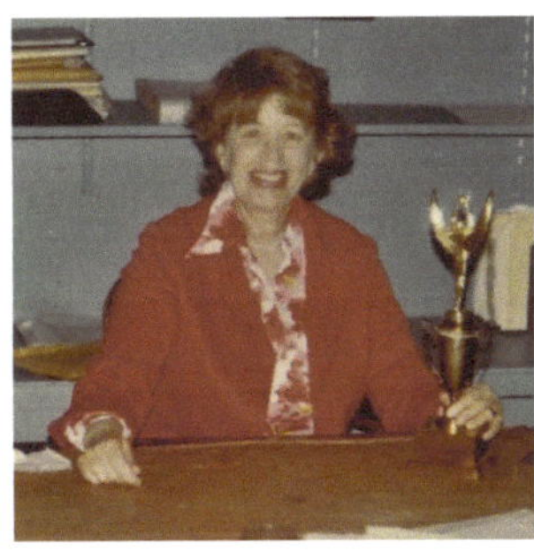

Age 9
THE QUEEN HAS ARRIVED!
My daughter is a poet,
philosopher, and teacher.
She is the Princess & Pea!
BEAUTY & BRAINS!
LOVE & XOXO
MOMMY

What Do Books Do?

BOOKS ARE POWERFUL

Books Educate!
Books Enlighten!
Books Empower!
Books Emancipate!
Books Entertain!
Books Spring Eternal!
Books Drive Exploration!
Books Spark Evolution!
Books Ignite Revolution!

Sharon Esther Lampert

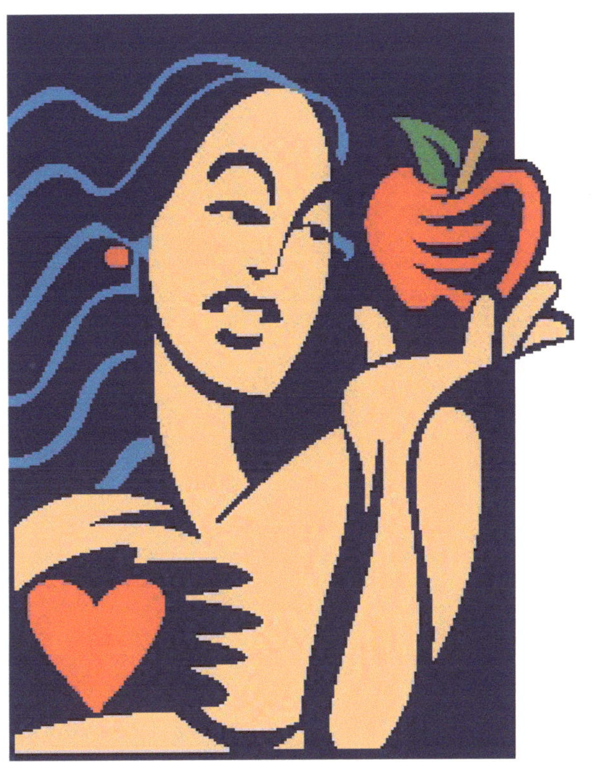

Through the Eyes of Eve

POETRY WORLD RECORD

120 Words of Rhyme From One Family of Rhyme

Sharon Esther Lampert

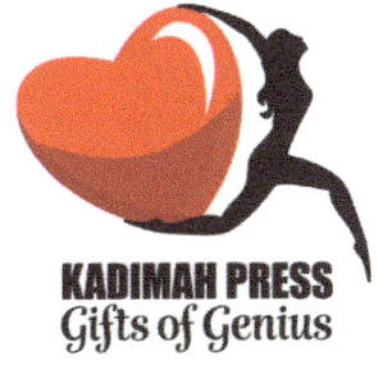

KADIMAH PRESS
Gifts of Genius

LITERATURE IS POWERFUL BEYOND WORDS FOR IT CREATES WORLDS

Sharon Esther Lampert

Bible Zone: Dvar Torah

Princess Kadimah's Interpretation of Adam and Eve

1. God creates the world and separates light from darkness, day from night, evening from morning, rivers from earth, sky, seasons, days and years.

2. God creates Adam and Eve, and they are living in the Garden of Eden or in God's womb and they are attached by God's umbilical cord, and God has to give birth to them (separate). When Eve eats the fruit, she has reached maturity, and it is time for God to give birth to Adam and Eve, to separate from them. Adam and Eve exit God's womb to serve God and continue the creation.

Poetry Reviews

"Forevermore, this POETRY WORLD RECORD of 120 rhymes from one family of rhyme will be unchallengeable for generations to come: poetry segues into philosophy, comedy, and Biblical scholarship. There is a universal message of knowns and unknowns for all people of all ages; and a reinterpretation of the text, the drama between Adam and Eve that finally sets Eve free from misogyny. Eve is now a liberated woman. This poem is a literary gift from GOD:GENIUS."

R. Levine, Teacher

"Through The Eyes of Eve"
A Poetic Classic,
Deeply Philosophical,
Eternally Feminine,
Biblical & Modern,
Melodious, Mystical,
Scholarly and, Oh (Oy),
So Very Humorous,
JUST DIVINE!"
—E Paikoff

"Also, that's good to hear about Eve. I was waiting for someone to do that!"
Brian Henry

Stanza One: Gift of Eve
Stanza Two: Forbidden Fruit
Stanza Three: Eve's Gift
Stanza Four: Serpent
Stanza Five: Adam Eats Fruit
Stanza Six: Adam Blames Eve
Stanza Seven: The Exile
Stanza Eight: Eve's Gift of Childbirth
Stanza Nine: Adam and Eve's Gift (SEX)
Stanza Ten: Future Generations

Yiddish Translations:
Oy: interjection means "worry"
Oy Vai Iz Mir: "woe is me"

Through the Eyes of Eve

Sharon Esther Lampert

GOD Gave Adam the Gift of Eve (Genesis 2:18);
GOD Gave Eve the Gift of Life (Genesis 2:20).

(1) Foreshown

GOD Knowingly gave to Adam alone

the gift of UNknown Eve of clone

to be sewn from Adam's gift of bone

for his very own (Oy, a wishbone)

(Genesis 2:18-23)

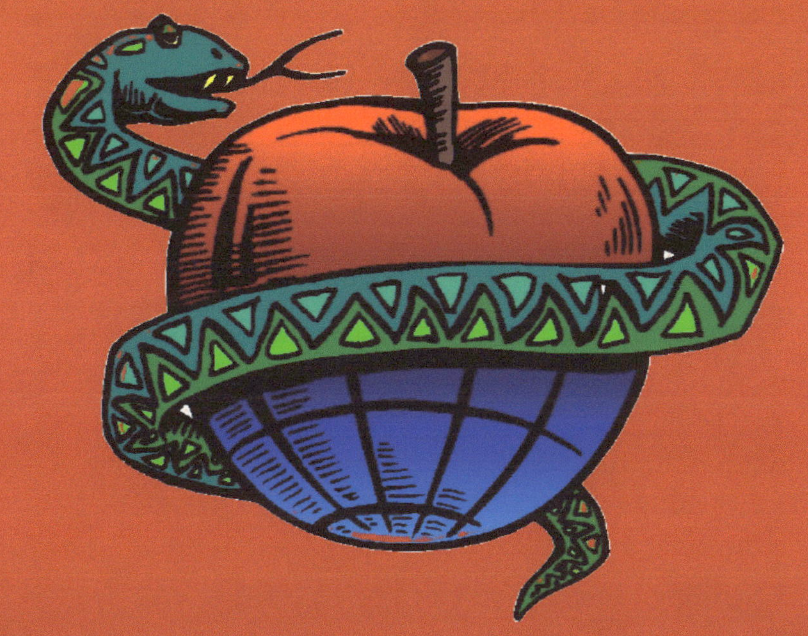

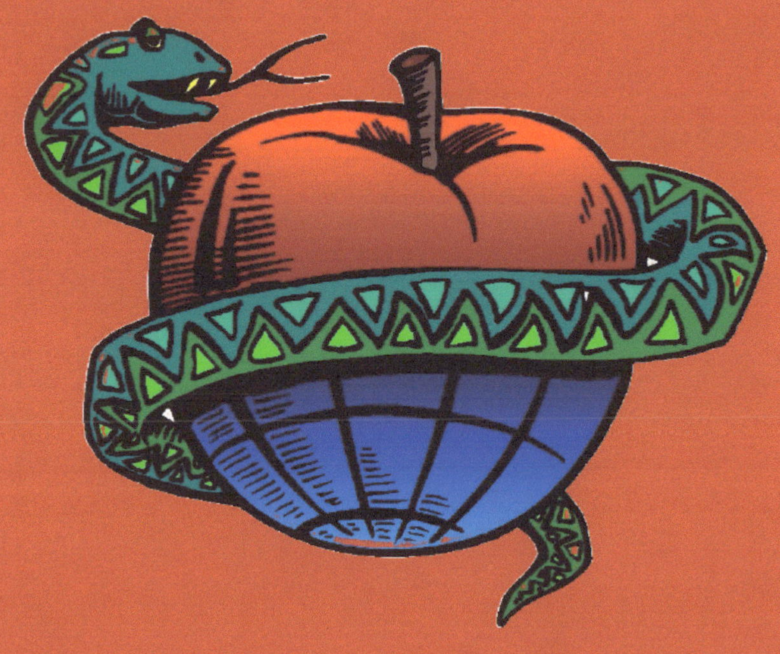

(2) GOD spoke to Adam

about that **UNKnown**,

forbidden tree of Knowledge of Good and Evil,

full-grown, a **Known** safety zone (Oy, a danger zone of clingstones)

(Genesis 2:16).

(3) **ForeKnown** (Oy, tales without a tailbone)

good or bad, the serpent **Knowingly** Knew, that

Eve's interpretation of what GOD had said was matter of fact, untrue;

UNKnowingly, through the serpent's eyes, eating the fruit to Eve's

surprise, would not be her demise (Oy, the matriarch known was not to

be dethroned)

(Genesis 3:1-5).

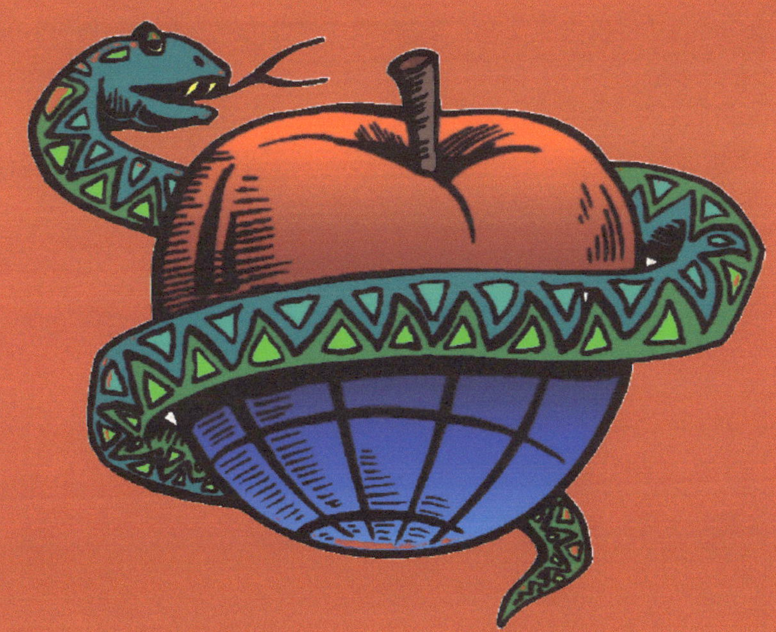

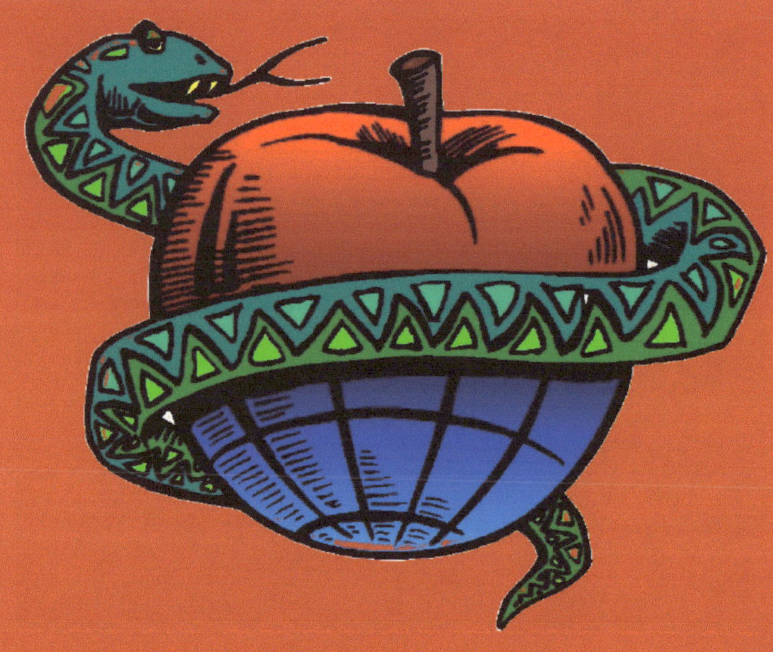

(4) In the eyes of Eve,

outgrown, with a bigger breastbone (Oy, silicone)

ingrown, it was instinctively Known, UNKnowingly childbearing prone,

that feeding and eating were good for Knowledge (Oy, gotta graduATE

college) (Genesis 3:6),

as GOD Knowingly gave to Eve alone

the gift to be the she-bearer of the womb of life, as shown

(Genesis 3:20).

(5) In the eyes of Eve,

UNKnowingly naked . . . Adam ate

fruit UNbeKnown (Oy, a crazy bone), full of secrets, Known to

be sacred (Oy, bemoan, a kidney stone) and (Oy, begroan, a

gallstone)

(Genesis 3:6).

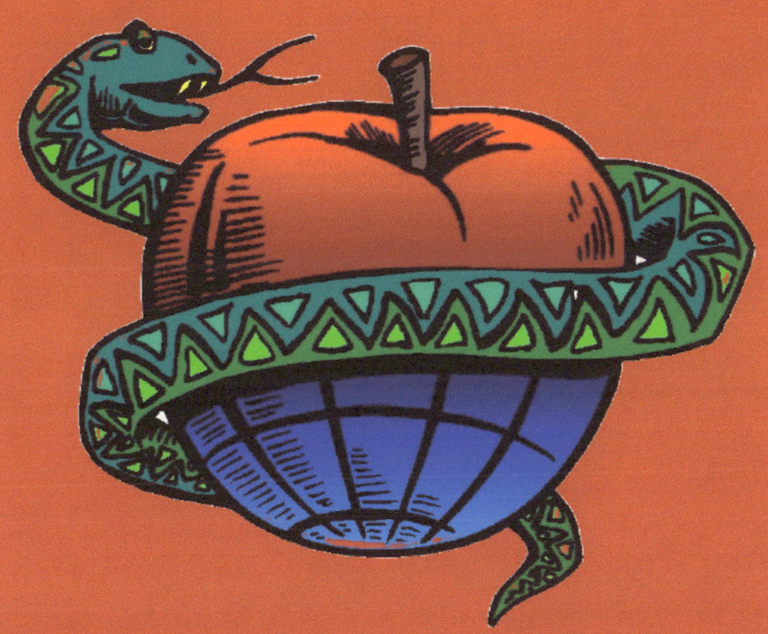

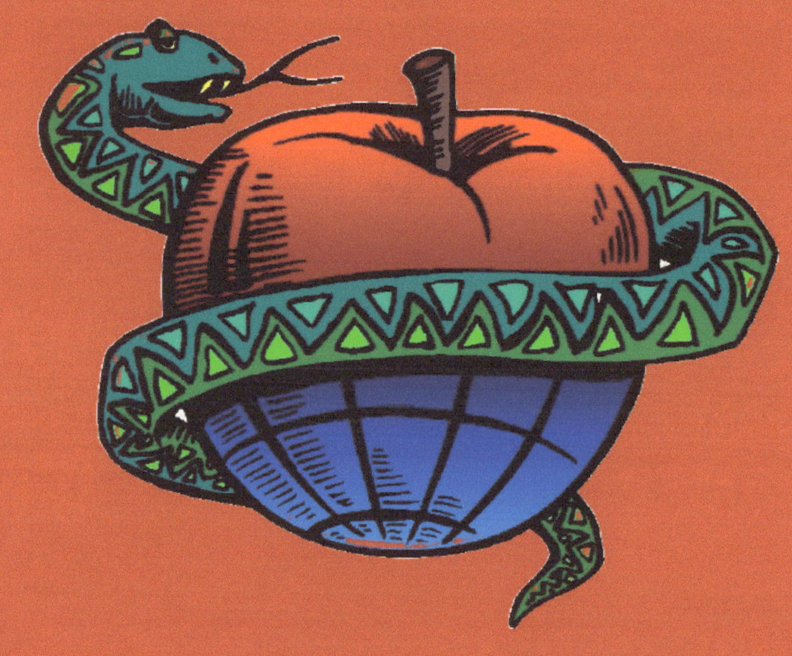

(6) In the eyes of Adam,

on his own, his behavior **Known**, (Oy, a poor retinal cone)

Eve was **Unknowingly** blamed (Oy, a jagged jawbone) and disowned,

Eve was on her own "sticks and stones may break my bones, but

names... I married a doggone knucklebone" (Oy, a combat zone)

(Genesis 3:12).

(7) In the eyes of GOD,

Adam did not acKnowledge his Known misdeed

for a commandment intoned, that he had Known, and must atone,

(Oy, poor earphones), out of tune and out of tone, monotone, if only he

had known! OY, a CYCLONE of hailstones "fire and brimstones"; cause

GOD has no funny bone (Genesis 3:17-19)

. . . Unknowingly rezoned (Oy, an eroding ozone)

Adam tiller of the Garden of Eden (Oy, a tropical zone)

well Known is overthrown to till (Oy, my backbone),

the overblown soil of an overgrown windblown, grass-grown garden

Unknown (Oy, the grindstone):

fieldstone, sandstone, millstone, cobblestone, soapstone, drystone,

ironstone, and limestone are RESEWN with firestone and paving stone

into capstone, cornerstone, copestone, curbstone, foundation stone, and

brownstone, Oy, Adam's aching shoulder bone, hipbone, thighbone,

knee bone, anklebone, chinbone, and shinbone (Oy, muscle tone)

(Genesis 3:23).

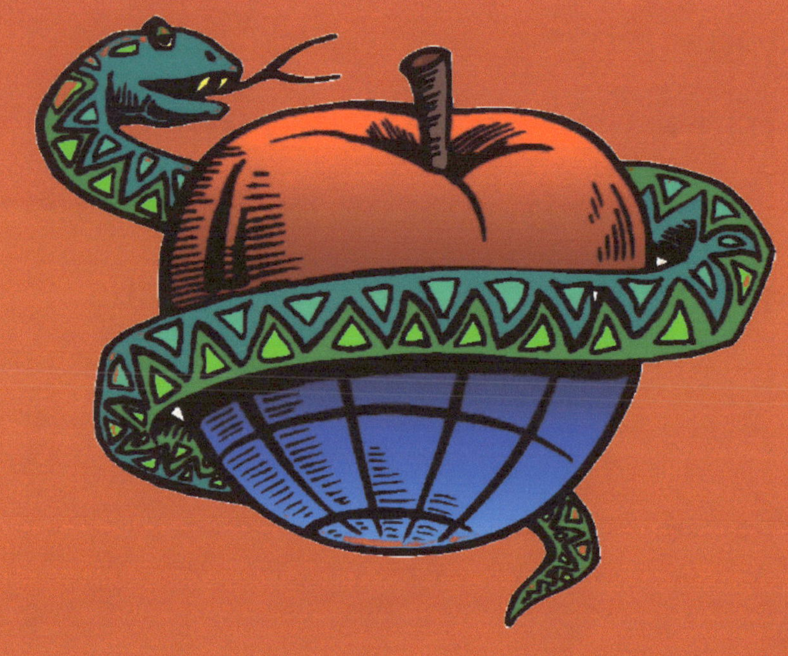

(8) GOD gave Eve

of her very own (Oy, Adam was outshone) the Known joyful gift of a

pubic bone, for Unknown painful childbirth, holding her own, groan,

a milestone (Oy, phenobarbitone)

(Genesis 3:16).

(9) Adam and Eve gave to Each Other (Oy, hormones of progesterone and testosterone) the known cheekbone (Oy, seductive eau de cologne, and a gramophone playing a saxaphone) of homegrown unforbidden immense sexual passion unchaperoned (Oy, Oy, ALONE) and UnforeKnowingly, unforeseen orgasmic pleasures unforetold Oy, Oy, PHERO-MOANS (Genesis 4:1).
Enthroned, Adam gave Eve a well Known precious stone, a glistening gemstone, not made of Unknown birthstone, cinnamon stone, moonstone, toadstone or rhinestone (Oy, a touchstone).

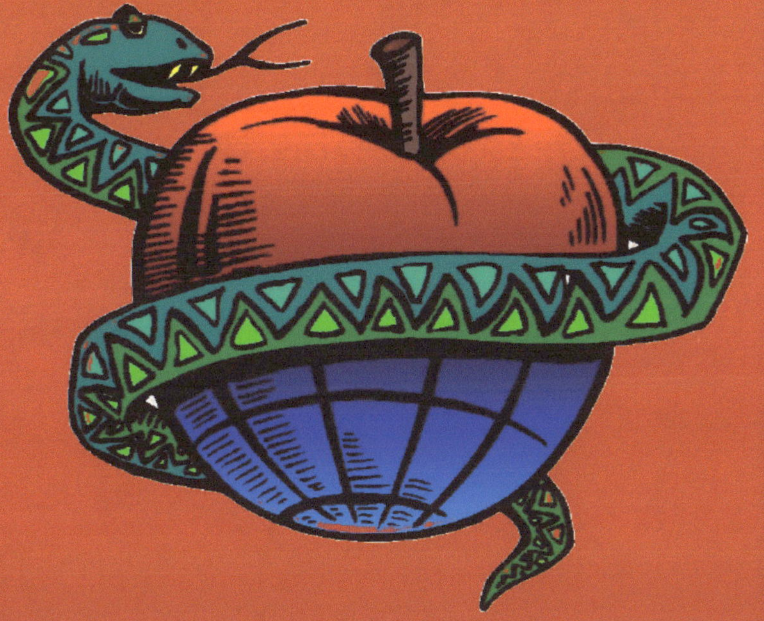

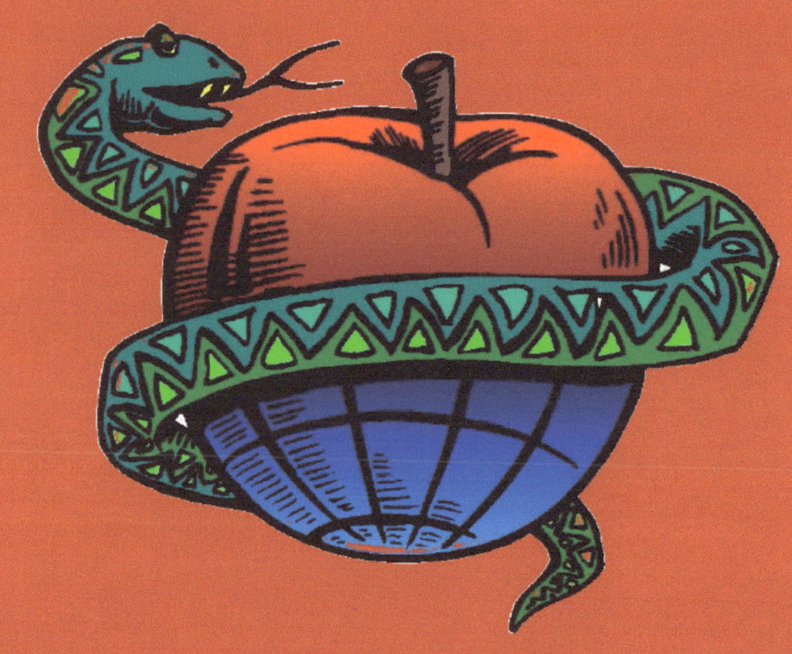

(10) Adam and Eve gave GOD
Future Generations of **KNOWN** (Oy, a microphone) and
well known (Oy, a megaphone) and unknown, no speakerphone or
dialtone on the telephone or cellphone (Oy, postponed, Oy, Oy, Oy Vai Iz Mir!
"DUST to dust" gifts, a loan; and a gravestone [Oy, a tombstone of headstone or footstone?] of knowing -a stepping stone- (Oy, a rosetta stone or
philosophers' stone) and unknowing -on their own- (Oy, accident prone)
(Genesis 5:1).

To Be Continued . . .

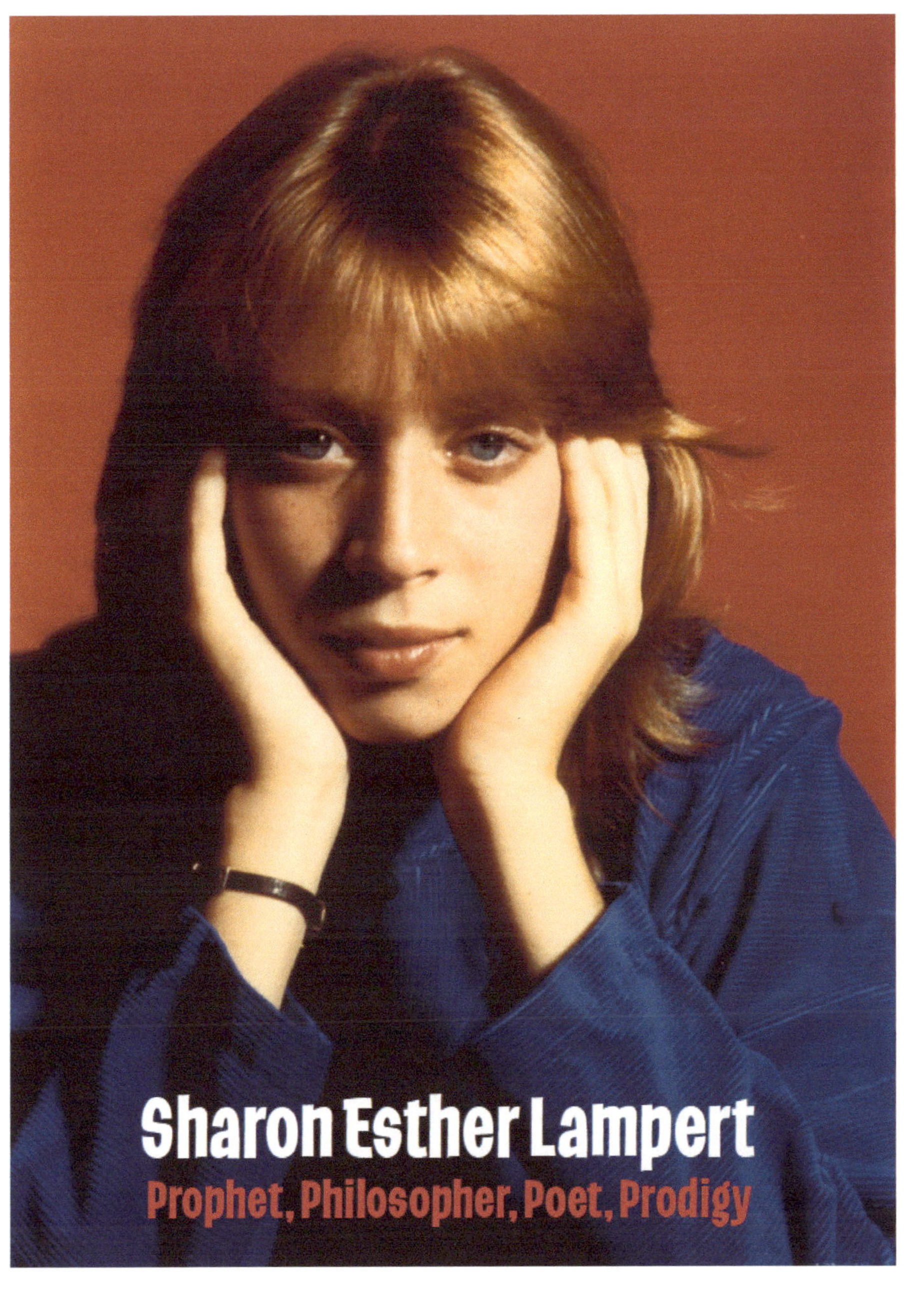

NO FAKES
NO FLOPS
NO FILLER
NO FLUFF
NO FUDGE
NO FAT
NO F-BOMB

©SharonEstherLampert.com

Stanza One: Gift of Eve
Stanza Two: Forbidden Fruit
Stanza Three: Eve's Gift
Stanza Four: Serpent
Stanza Five: Adam Eats Fruit
Stanza Six: Adam Blames Eve
Stanza Seven: The Exile
Stanza Eight: Eve's Gift of Childbirth
Stanza Nine: Adam and Eve's Gift (SEX)
Stanza Ten: Future Generations

Yiddish Translations:
Oy: interjection means "worry"
Oy Vai Iz Mir: "woe is me"

Original Poem: 2008
Through the Eyes of Eve
By Sharon Esther Lampert

(1) Foreshown
GOD knowingly gave to Adam alone
the gift of unknown Eve of clone
to be sewn from Adam's gift of bone
for his very own (Oy, a wishbone) (Genesis 2:18-23).

(2) GOD spoke to Adam
about that unknown, forbidden tree of Knowledge of Good and
Evil, full-grown, a known safety zone (Oy, a danger zone of clingstones) (Genesis 2:16).

(3) Foreknown (Oy, tales without a tailbone)
good or bad, the serpent knowingly Knew, that
Eve's interpretation of what GOD had said was matter of fact, untrue;
unknowingly, through the serpent's eyes, eating the fruit to Eve's surprise, would
not be her demise (Oy, the matriarch known was not to be dethroned) (Genesis 3:1-5).

(4) In the eyes of Eve,
outgrown, with a bigger breastbone (Oy, silicone)
ingrown, it was instinctively Known, unknowingly childbearing prone, that feeding and
eating were good for Knowledge (Oy, gotta graduATE college) (Genesis 3:6),
as GOD knowingly gave to Eve alone
the gift to be the she-bearer of the womb of life, as shown (Genesis 3:20).
In the eyes of Eve, unknowingly naked . . . Adam ate
fruit unbeknown (Oy, a crazy bone), full of secrets, known to be sacred
(Oy, bemoan, a kidney stone) and (Oy, begroan, a gallstone) (Genesis 3:6).

(5) In the eyes of Eve,
unknowingly naked . . . Adam ate
fruit unbeknown (Oy, a crazy bone), full of secrets, known to
be sacred (Oy, bemoan, a kidney stone) and (Oy, begroan, a gallstone)
(Genesis 3:6).

(6) In the eyes of Adam,
on his own, his behavior Known, (Oy, a poor retinal cone)
Eve was unknowingly blamed (Oy, a jagged jawbone) and disowned,
Eve was on her own "sticks and stones may break my bones, but
names... I married a doggone knucklebone" (Oy, a combat zone)
(Genesis 3:12).

(7) In the eyes of GOD,
Adam did not acKnowledge his known misdeed
for a commandment intoned, that he had known, and must atone,
(Oy, poor earphones), out of tune and out of tone, monotone, if only he
had known! OY, a CYCLONE of hailstones "fire and brimstones"; cause
GOD has no funny bone (Genesis 3:17-19)
. . . unknowingly rezoned (Oy, an eroding ozone)
Adam tiller of the Garden of Eden (Oy, a tropical zone)
well known is overthrown to till (Oy, my backbone),
the overblown soil of an overgrown windblown, grass-grown garden
unknown (Oy, the grindstone):
fieldstone, sandstone, millstone, cobblestone, soapstone, drystone, ironstone,
and limestone are RESEWN with firestone and paving stone into
capstone, cornerstone, copestone, curbstone, foundation stone, and
brownstone, OY, Adam's aching shoulder bone, hipbone, thighbone, knee
bone, anklebone, chinbone, and shinbone (Oy, muscle tone)
(Genesis 3:23).

(8) GOD gave Eve
of her very own (Oy, Adam was outshone) the Known joyful gift of a
pubic bone, for UNKnown painful childbirth, holding her own, groan,
a milestone (Oy, phenobarbitone)
(Genesis 3:16).

(9) Adam and Eve gave to Each Other (Oy, hormones of progesterone
and testosterone) the known cheekbone (Oy, seductive eau de
cologne, and a gramophone playing a saxaphone) of homegrown
unforbidden immense sexual passion unchaperoned (Oy, Oy, ALONE)
and unforeknowingly, unforeseen orgasmic pleasures
unforetold Oy, Oy, PHERO-MOANS (Genesis 4:1).
Enthroned, Adam gave Eve a well Known precious stone,
a glistening gemstone, not made of
unknown birthstone, cinnamon stone, moonstone,
toadstone or rhinestone (Oy, a touchstone).

(10) Adam and Eve gave GOD
Future Generations of known (Oy, a microphone) and well known (Oy, a megaphone) and
unknown, no speakerphone or dialtone on the telephone or cellphone (Oy, postponed, Oy, Oy, Oy
Vai Iz Mir! "DUST to dust" gifts, a loan; and a gravestone [Oy, a tombstone of headstone or footstone?]
of knowing -a stepping stone- (Oy, a rosetta stone or philosophers' stone) and unknowing - on their
own - (Oy, accident prone)
(Genesis 5:1).

To Be Continued . . .

POETRY WORLD RECORD
120 Words of Rhyme From One Family of Rhyme

Stanza One: Gift of Eve
1. foreshown
2. alone
3. unknown
4. clone
5. sewn
6. bone
7. own (kabbalistic significance)
8. wishbone (kabbalistic significance)

Stanza Two: Forbidden Fruit
9. full grown
10. known (kabbalistic significance)
11. safety zone
12. danger zone
13. clingstones

Stanza Three: Eve's Gift
14. foreknown
15. tailbone
    another rhyme: knew, untrue
    another rhyme: eyes, surprise, demise
16. dethroned

Stanza Four: Serpent
17. outgrown
18. breastbone (kabbalistic significance)
19. silicone
20. ingrown
21. prone
    another rhyme: eating, feeding
    another rhyme: knowledge, college
22. shown (kabbalistic significance)

Stanza Five: Adam Eats Fruit
another rhyme: naked, sacred
23. unbeknown
24. crazybone
25. bemoan
26. kidney stone
27. begroan
28. gallstone

Stanza Six: Adam Blames Eve
29. retinal cone
30. jawbone
31. disown
32. sticks and stones may break my bones
33. doggone
    (kabbalistic significance)
34. knucklebone
35. combat zone

Stanza Seven: The Exile

36. intoned
37. atone
38. earphone
39. tone
40. monotone (kabbalistic significance)
41. cyclone
42. hailstone
43. brimstone
44. funny bone
45. rezoned
46. ozone
47. tropical zone
48. well known
49. overthrown
50. backbone
51. overblown
52. overgrown
53. windblown
54. grass-grown
55. grindstone
56. fieldstone
57. sandstone
58. millstone
59. cobblestone
60. soapstone
61. dryston
62. ironstone
63. limestone
64. resewn
65. firestone
66. paving stone
67. capstone
68. cornerstone
69. copestone
70. curbstone
71. foundation stone
72. brownstone
73. shoulder bone
74. hipbone
75. thighbone
76. knee bone
77. anklebone
78. chinbone
79. shinbone
80. muscle tone

Stanza Eight: Eve's Gift of Childbirth

81. outshone
82. pubic bone
83. groan
84. milestone
85. phenobarbitone

Stanza Nine: Adam and Eve's Gift (SEX)

86. hormone
87. progesterone
88. testosterone
89. cheekbone
90. eau de cologne
91. gramophone
92. saxaphone
93. homegrown
94. unchaperoned
95. phero-moans
96. enthroned
97. precious stone
98. gemstone
99. birthstone
100. cinnamon stone
101. moonstone
102. toadstone
103. rhinestone
104. touchstone

Stanza Ten: Future Generations

105. microphone
106. megaphone
107. speakerphone
108. dialtone
109. cellphone
110. telephone
111. postpone
112. loan
113. gravestone
114. tombstone
115. headstone
116. footstone
117. stepping stone
118. rosetta stone
119. philosopher's stone
120. accident prone

Philosophy Zone

Known and UnKnown

Stanza One: Adam's Gift of Eve
- Known: God
- Unknown: Eve

Stanza Two: Forbidden Fruit
- Known: Tree of Life
- Unknown: forbidden fruit

Stanza Three: Serpent
- Known: serpent
- Unknown: Eve

Stanza Four: God's Gift to Eve
- Known: God
- Unknown: childbearing

Stanza Five: Adam Eats Fruit
- Known: sacred secrets
- Unknown: fruit

Stanza Six: "Combat Zone"
- Known: Adam's behavior
- Unknown: Eve is blamed

Stanza Seven: The Exile
- Well Known: Garden of Eden
- Known: Commandment
- Unknown: Adam is rezoned

Stanza Eight: Eve's Gift
- Known: joyful children
- Unknown: painful childbirth

Stanza Nine: Adam and Eve's Gift
- Known: sexual passion
- Unknown: orgasmic pleasure
- Well Known: glistening gemstone
- Unknown: stones

Stanza Ten: Future Generations
- Well Known: megaphone
- Known: mircrophone
- Unknown: accident prone

Literary Contribution to World Literature

POETRY WORLD RECORD

"Through The Eyes of Eve"

1. **POETRY WORLD RECORD: 120 WORDS OF RHYME FROM ONE FAMILY OF RHYME**

2. There is a reinterpretation of the text, the drama between Adam and Eve that finally sets Eve free from 5000 years of misogyny – Eve is now a liberated woman!

3. Poem travels from the origins of creation to the present day (Oy!)

4. Poetry segues into philosophy, comedy, Biblical scholarship, and Biblical interpretation.

5. Poetry is interwoven with philosophy and very funny Yiddish comedy.

6. Philosophy: in each stanza, there is a universal message of **KNOWNS** and **UNKNOWNS.**

7. Biblical Scholarship: poem directly addresses and footnotes verses from the Bible.

8. The poem sets an unchallengeable **WORLD RECORD OF 120 WORDS OF RHYME**

8. Metaphysical Inspiration: GOD has to be with you to break this **POETRY WORLD RECORD**

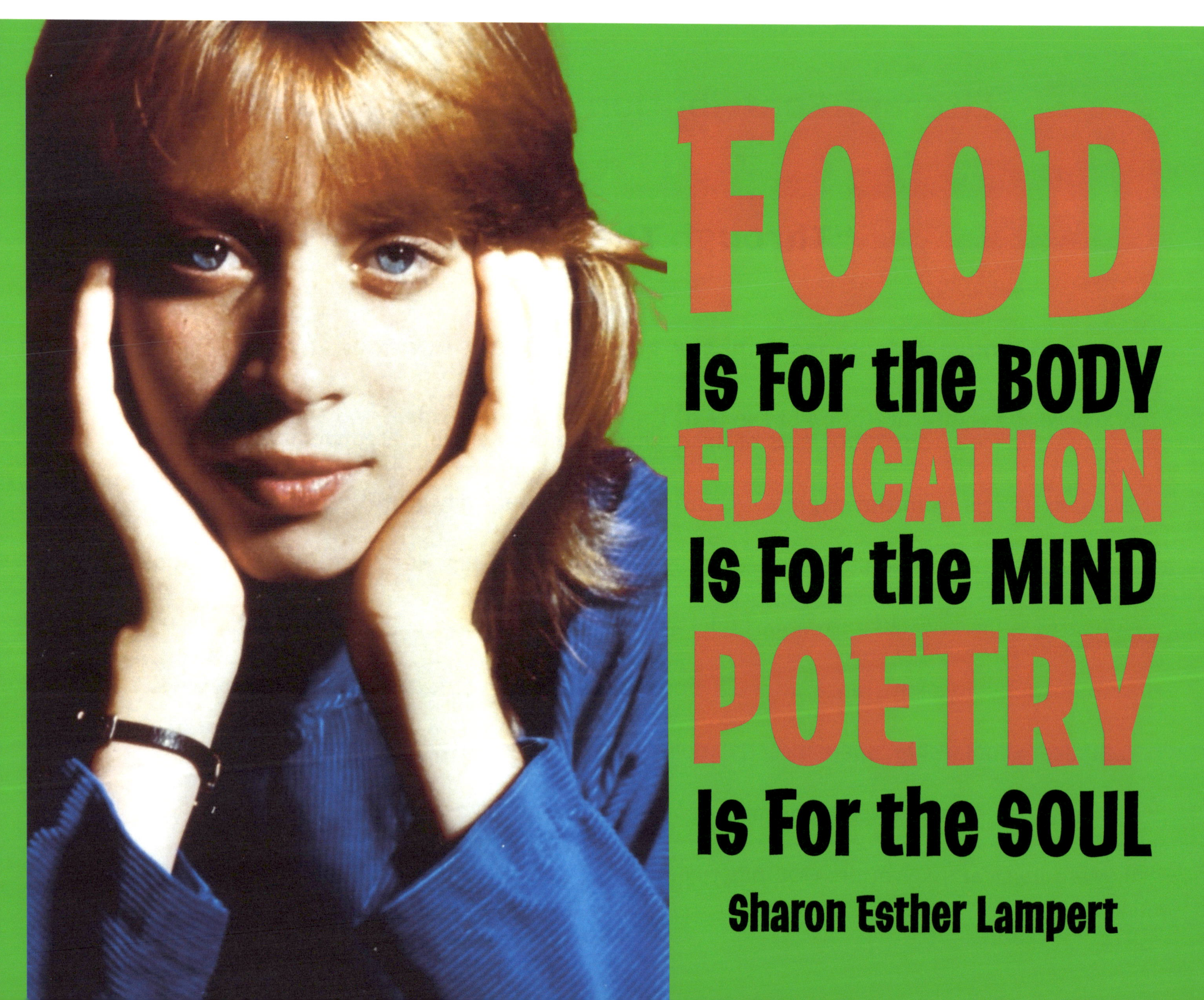

FOOD
Is For the BODY
EDUCATION
Is For the MIND
POETRY
Is For the SOUL
Sharon Esther Lampert

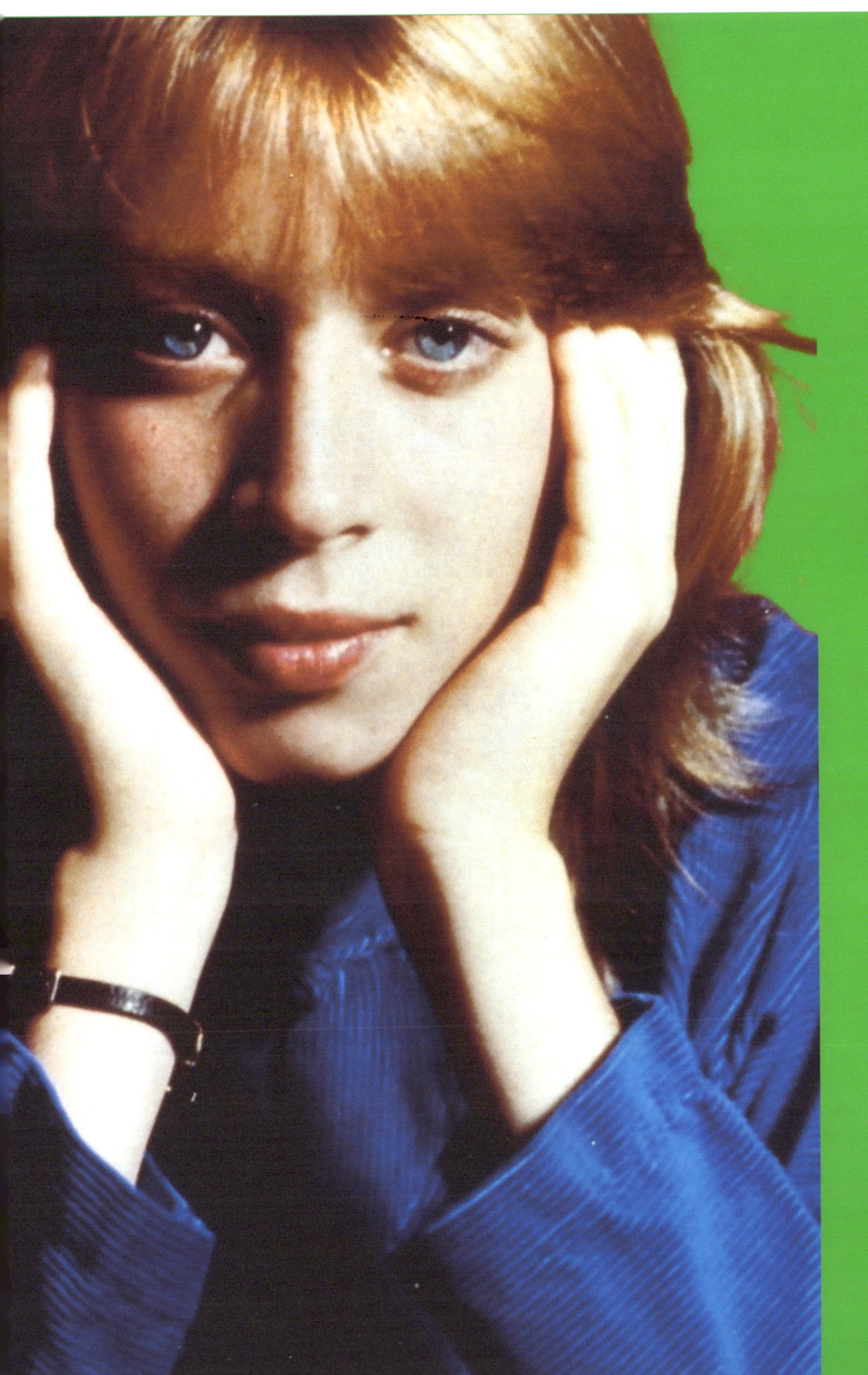

MY Life Is an OPEN Book to KNOW Me Is to READ Me

Sharon Esther Lampert

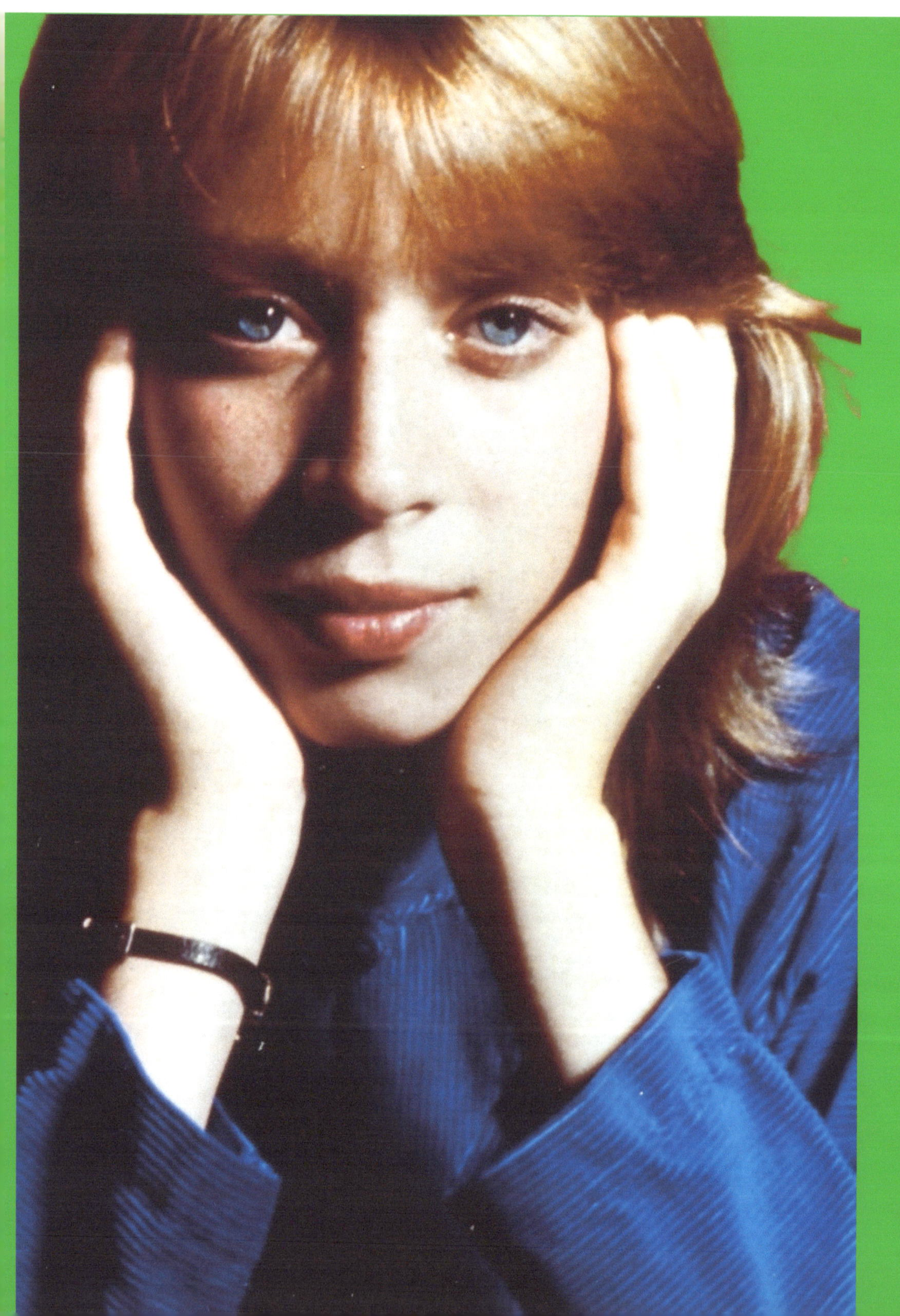

The SOLE Intention of My POETRY Is to Add LIGHT to Your SOUL

Sharon Esther Lampert

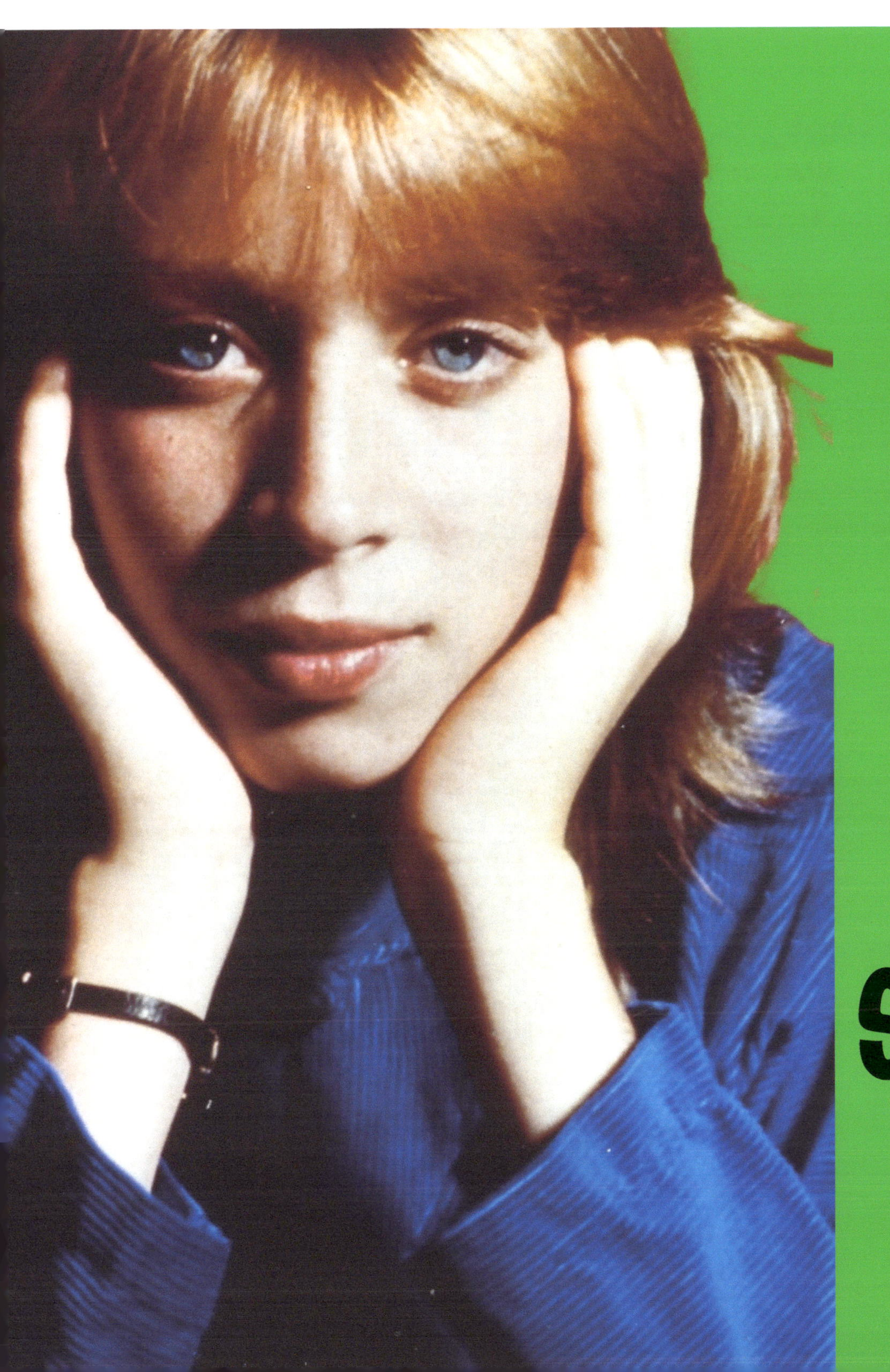

Poetry Is
Contagious
Spread the
Word...
Stay Home
Write Verse
Save Lives and
Literature

Sharon Esther Lampert

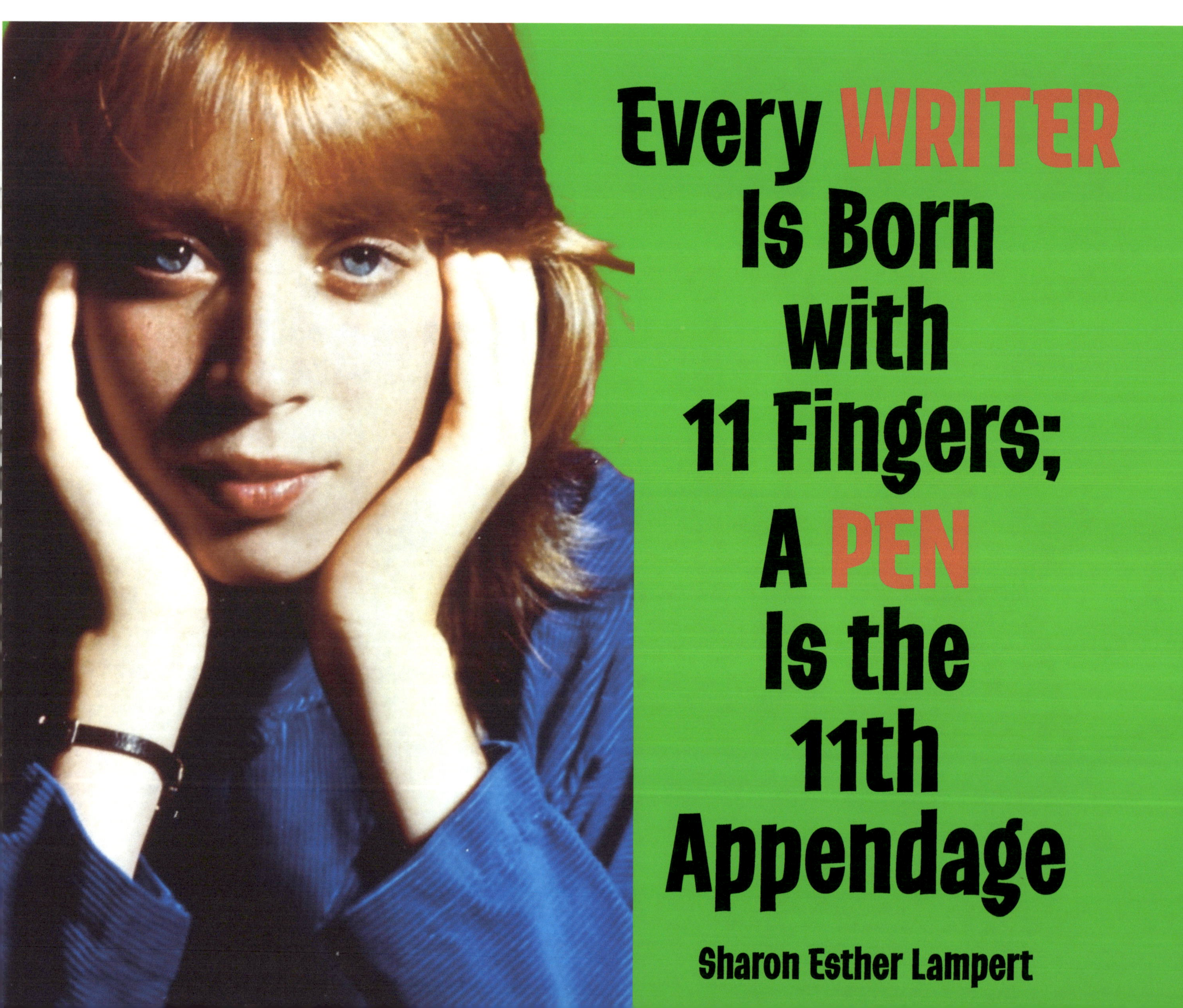

Every WRITER
Is Born
with
11 Fingers;
A PEN
Is the
11th
Appendage
Sharon Esther Lampert

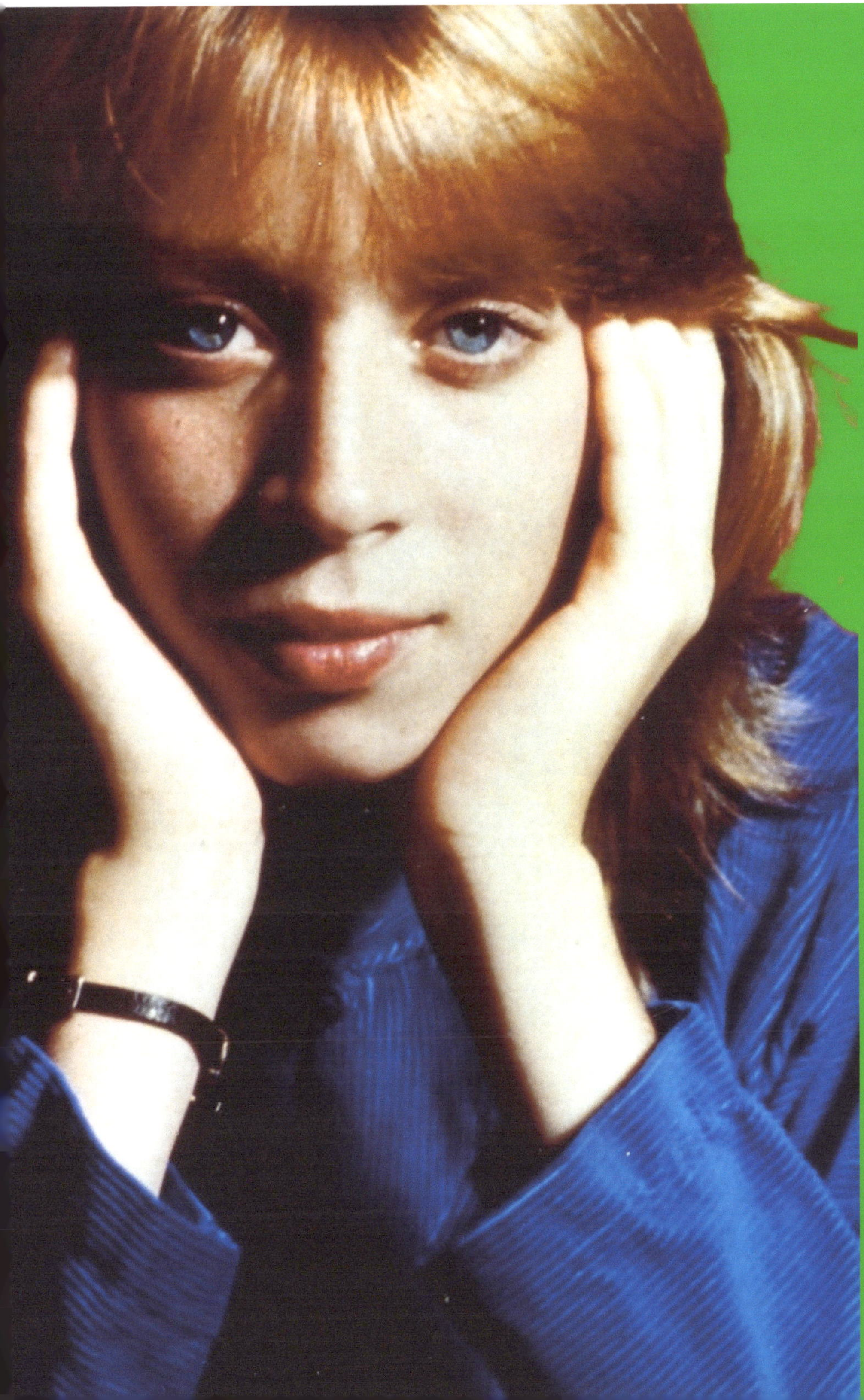

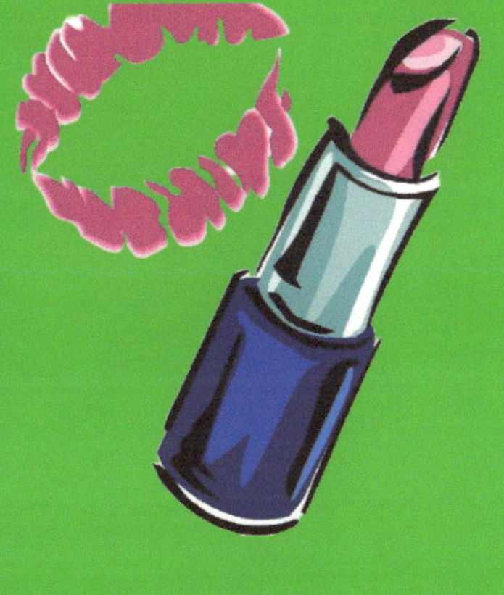

Do you
want me
to sign it
in
INK
or
in
LIPSTICK?
Sharon Esther Lampert

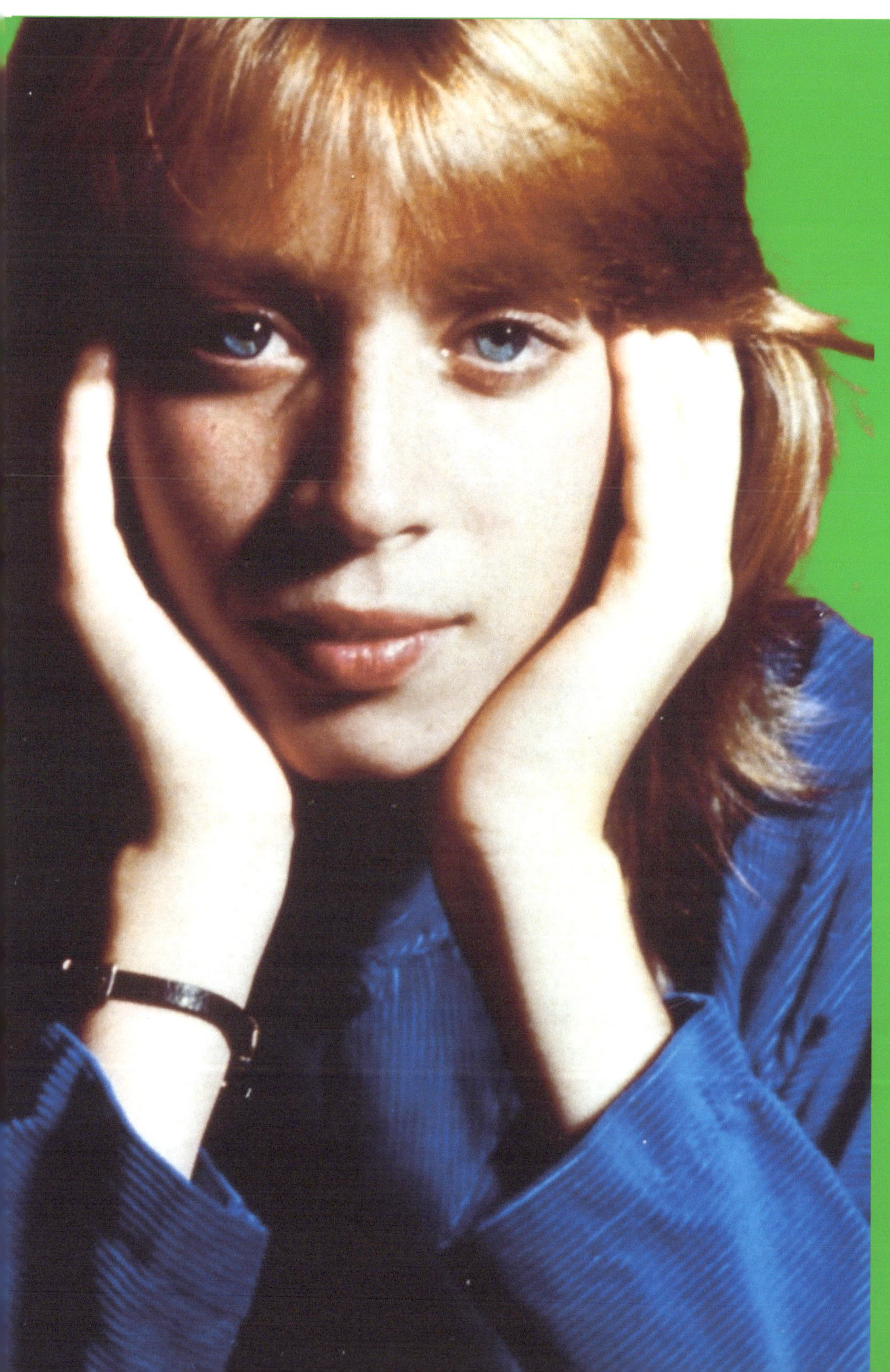

GIFT OF GENIUS

ONE GREAT POEM
IS LUCKY

TWO GREAT POEMS
mean I have something
but I don't know what it is

THREE GREAT POEMS
mean I have something,
and I have to learn to
work at it, but there is
no instruction manual

FORTY GREAT POEMS
mean I have a gift, and
the gift is a mystery

Sharon Esther Lampert

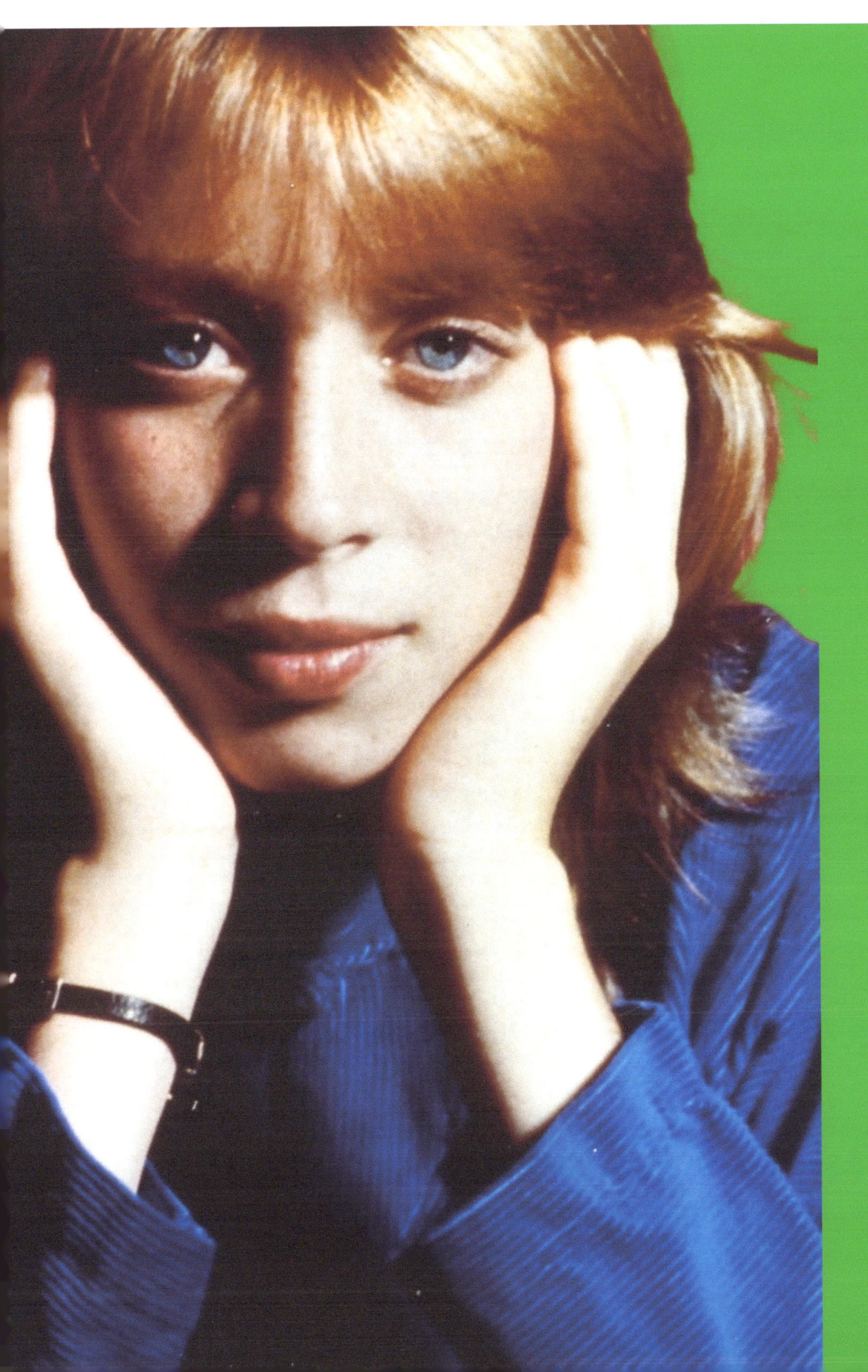

My Books Are My Remains; Please Handle Them Gently

Sharon Esther Lampert

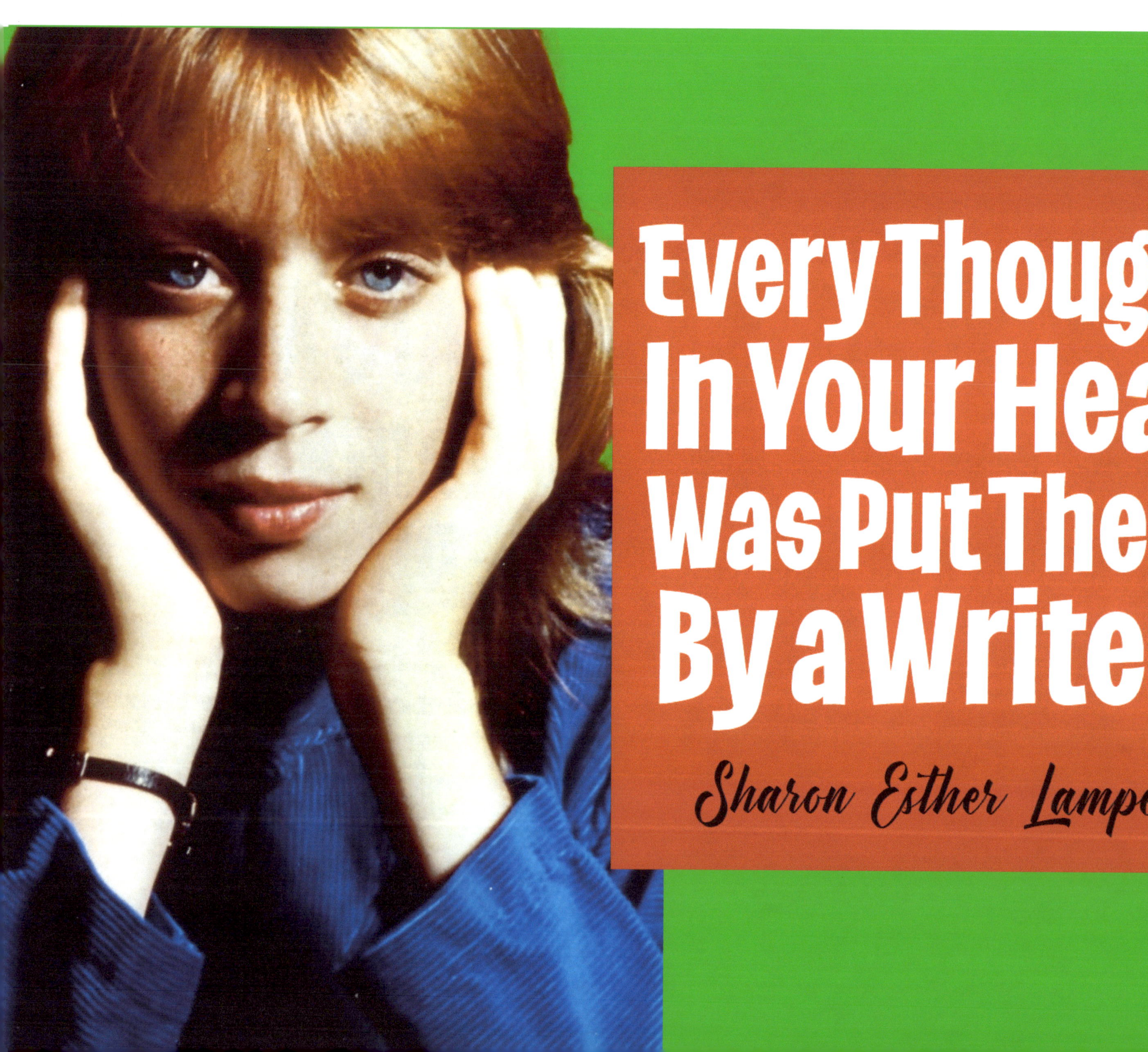

Every Thought In Your Head Was Put There By a Writer!
Sharon Esther Lampert

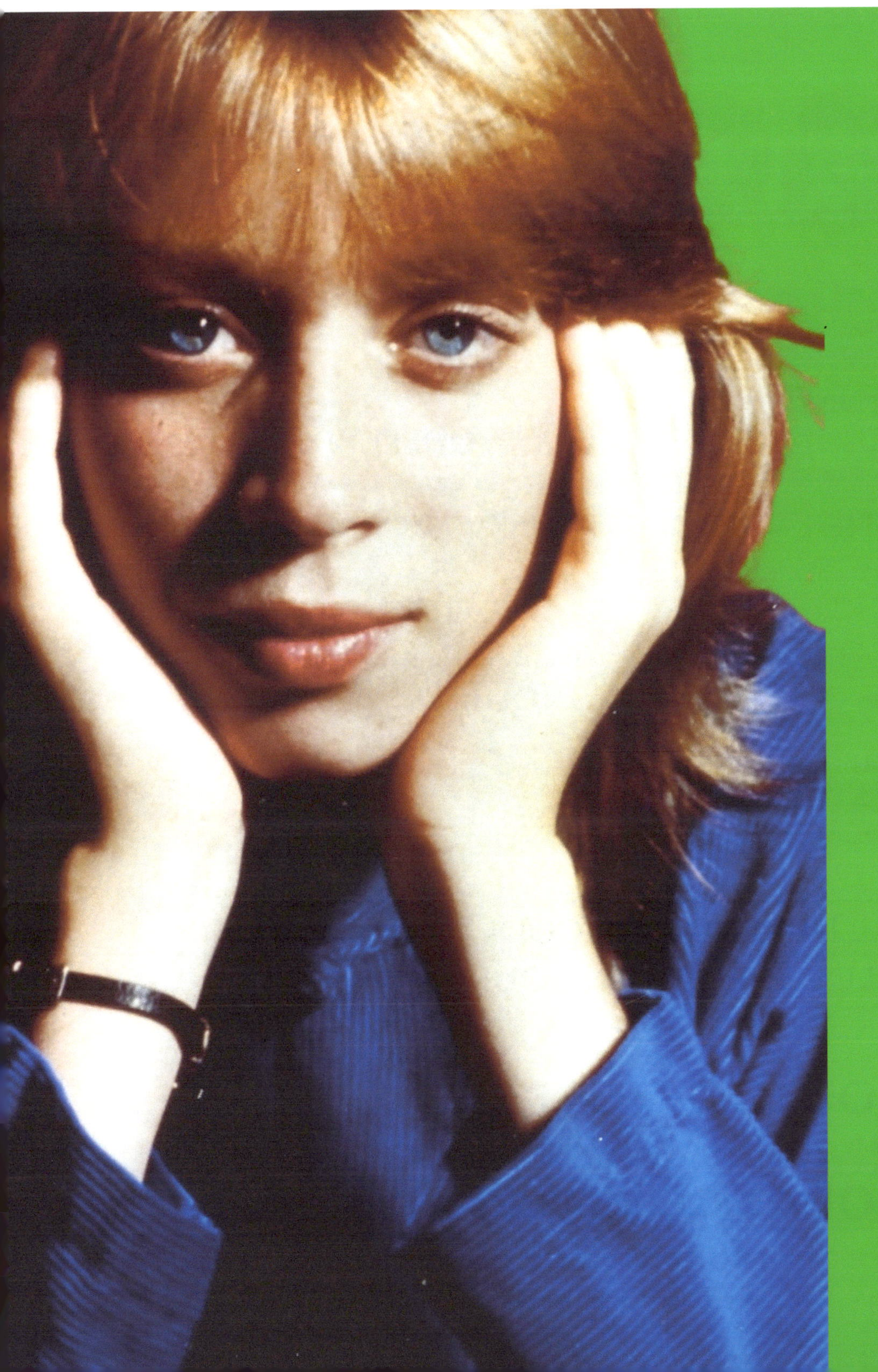

Please don't let me DIE with a TYPO!

Sharon Esther Lampert

GOD IS GO! DO!

1. Our World Is Organized by **LAWS OF INEXTRICABILITY**

2. THERE ARE TWO WORLDS:
A PHYSICAL WORLD AND A **METAPHYSICAL** WORLD

3. GOD IS NOT PHYSICS THE LAWS OF THE UNIVERSE
GOD IS METAPHYSICS

4. YOUR MIND, THOUGHTS, AND IDEAS ARE **INVISIBLE** AND **INTANGIBLE** ENTITIES
— BEYOND THE SCOPE OF SCIENTIFIC INQUIRY!

5. **GOD IS GO! DO!**
GOD CAN ONLY DO FOR YOU WHAT GOD CAN DO THROUGH YOU

6. **PRAY** AS IF IT ALL DEPENDS ON GOD!
WORK AS IF IT ALL DEPENDS ON YOU!

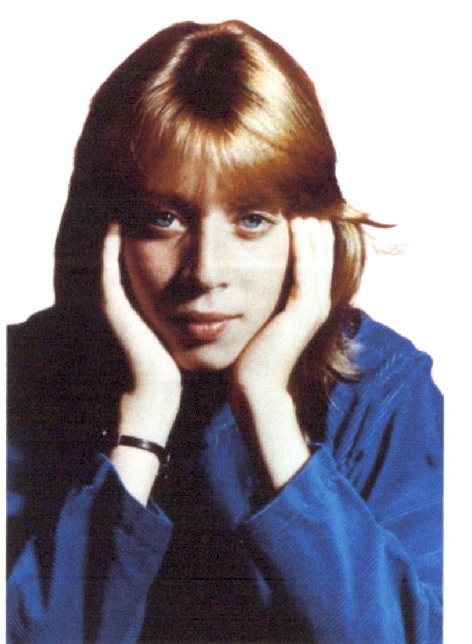

YOU HAD TO OUTDO MOSES!
THE 22 COMMANDMENTS
UNIVERSAL MORAL COMPASS

Prophet Sharon Esther Lampert

Q: Why Is It NORMAL for 8 Billion People to Talk to God but CRAZY If God Talks to Me?

First Edition Collectible

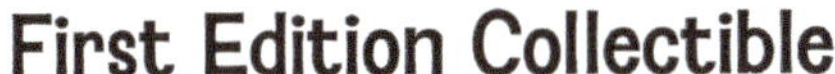

SHARON ESTHER LAMPERT
SEE THE WORLD THROUGH THE EYES OF A CREATIVE GENIUS
Poet, Prophet, Philosopher, Peacemaker, Prodigy

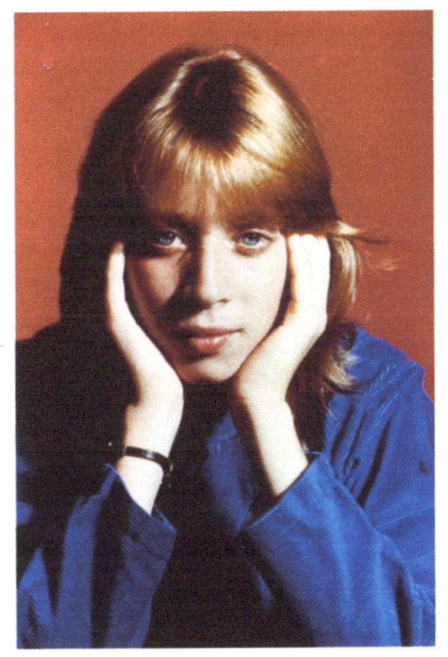

God Talks to Me
A Working Definition of God

What Happens When You Dress Up Albert Einstein as Marilyn Monroe?
SHARON ESTHER LAMPERT

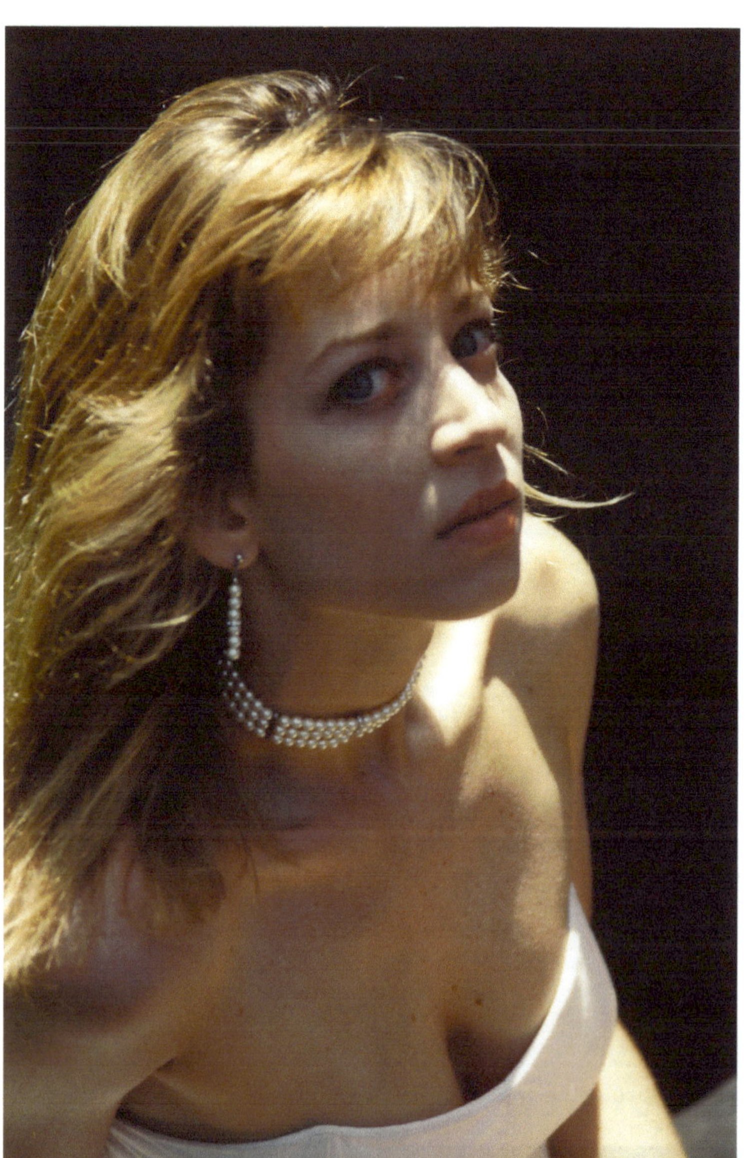

- Prodigy
- Poet
- Prophet
- Philosopher
- Peacemaker
- Paladin of Education
- **PHOTON SUPERHERO**
- Princess KADIMAH
- Princess & Pea
- Performer: Vocalist
- Player: Jock NYU Varsity B-Ball
- President
- Publisher
- Producer
- Psychobiologist:Rockefeller University
- Piano-Playing Cat
- Phoenix
- **PINUP**

WEBSITES
- SharonEstherLampert.com
- WorldFamousPoems.com
- PoetryJewels.com
- PhilosopherQueen.com
- GodIsGoDo.com
- Schmaltzy.com
- TrueLoveBurnsEternal.com
- SillyLittleBoys.com
- WinAtThin.com
- WritersRunTheWorld.com
- PalmBeachBookPublisher.com
- BooksArePowerful.com
- HappyGrandparenting.com
- WomenHaveAllThePower.com

EDUCATION
- Smartgrades.com
- PhotonSuperHero.com
- EveryDayAnEasyA.com
- BooksNotBombs.com

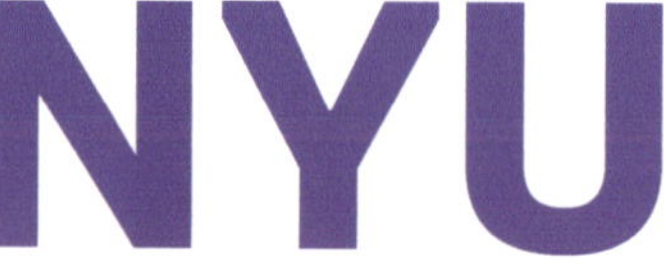

NYU
AWARD
for
"Multi-Interdisciplinary Studies"
YOUTUBE VIDEO

Honors & Awards

NYU AWARD
Multi-Interdisciplinary Studies
NYU 3 Degrees: BA, MA, MA
NYU Varsity Basketball Team
NYU Weightlifting Contest

NYC AWARD
100 Year Scholarship Award
Presented by NYC Mayor Koch

NY EMPIRE STATE AWARD
Math and Science Scholarship

JERUSALEM FELLOWSHIP
Aish Hatorah, Israel

ROCKEFELLER UNIVERSITY
Science Paper Publication

FIRST PRIZE
Upper East Side Resident
Newspaper Writing Contest

FIRST PRIZE
THE WAVE (1893) Art Contest

#1 POETRY WEBSITE
For Student Poetry Projects

POETRY WORLD RECORD
120 Words of Rhyme from
One Family of Rhyme

CONTRIBUTIONS TO CIVILIZATION
Scientist, Artist, Educator, Theologian

Published 80+ Books
NYU: PERSTARE et PRAESTARE

PRODIGY
10 Esoteric Laws of Genius and Creativity
Awesome Art of Alliteration Using One Letter of the Alphabet

PROPHET
GOD IS GO! DO!
22 COMMANDMENTS: A UNIVERSAL MORAL COMPASS -- NEW SCIENTIFIC THEORY!

PHYSICIST
LAWS OF INEXTRICABILITY - NEW SCIENTIFIC THEORY!

PSYCHOBIOLOGIST
THE SPERM MANIFESTO: 10 RULES FOR THE ROAD

PHILOSOPHER QUEEN
The Philosophy of Love
The Philosophy of Evil: THE DOUBLE WHAMMY
Women Have All The Power But Have Never Learned How to Use It

POET
WORLD POETRY RECORD
120 Words of Rhyme from One Family of Rhyme
#1 Poetry Website for Student Projects
The Greatest Poems Ever Written on Extraordinary World Events
The First Woman to Write a Book on 5000 Years of Jewish History

PALADIN OF EDUCATION
SMARTGRADES BRAIN POWER REVOLUTION
8 Goalposts of Education
40 Universal Gold Standards of Education
SCHMALTZY: The FIrst Book of Color-Coded Words
Learn to Read Hebrew in One Hour

PSYCHIATRIST
LOVE YOU MORE THAN YESTERDAY: 14 Relationship Strategies for Happily Ever After
Integration Therapy to Repair Broken-Winged Students
Monsters: Broken World of Broken People
Three Stages of Child Abuse
40 Rules of Manhood

PEACEMAKER
WORLD PEACE EQUATION

PINUP
SEXIEST GENIUS IN HUMAN HISTORY

True Story: Child Prodigy Meets Creative Genius

1.

Inspiration: 46 Words of Rhyme to 65 Words to 110 Words to 120 Words: "This poem was birthed by my first serious muse, J.M., nicknamed, "1001 Merabian Nights" and its first draft produced a poem with 46 words of rhyme.

2.

5 years passed. The second birthing and final birthing was catalyzed by my second serious muse, A.C., nicknamed "Israeli Miracle Grow." In one day, it grew to 65 words of rhyme and during the following weekend, it grew to 110 words and by the end of the weekend, it was 120 words of rhyme.

3.

Artistic Common Ground: "I have noticed that many artists comment on Adam and Eve, in painting and sculpture for reasons I don't understand.

4.

Academic Question: Does the poem really have 120 words or 121 words? (see phero-moan).
Academic Answer: "pheromone" and "moan" was made into a compound word that does not really exist, it is poetic license: "phero-moan." Is it two words based on two meanings interwoven into one word?

5.

First Day Out on the Town: Child Prodigy Meets Creative Genius
"I brought copies of the poem to the synagogue and handed them out to friends and fans and stated, matter of factly, that "I liberated Eve from 5000 years of misogyny and created a poetry world record." That same day, during Kiddish, I met once again a woman who it turned out is a child prodigy, having attended college at the age of 8. She read my poem, found a significant typo (a another internal drama as there is always a typo somewhere). She is also a poet and told me that although her brain in a super-human computer and she can probably break this record, she won't do it because she is my friend. Twenty-four hours had not even passed, and I had my very real first serious challenger to my POETRY WORLD RECORD. Child Prodigy Meets Creative Genius: I found myself feeling very cocky and I told her to go ahead and try if she think she can do it, but I doubt that she will be able to do so at the level that (I) created it, or the divine force or the "creative apparatus" within that keeps me company. She agreed with my analysis and that was that!

6.

As for the significant typo, found by my child-prodigy friend, I accidently wrote a word twice, "begroan" so that I only had 119 words, however, my friend Morry called the week before to let me know that I missed the word "telephone." When my child-prodigy friend found the typo, she also knew what word was missing, and so did I, thanks to Morry. So "telephone" was the 120th word added to the poem. Actually, later, I changed the word "moan" to "phero-moan."

7.

There is a very fine line between child prodigy and creative genius.

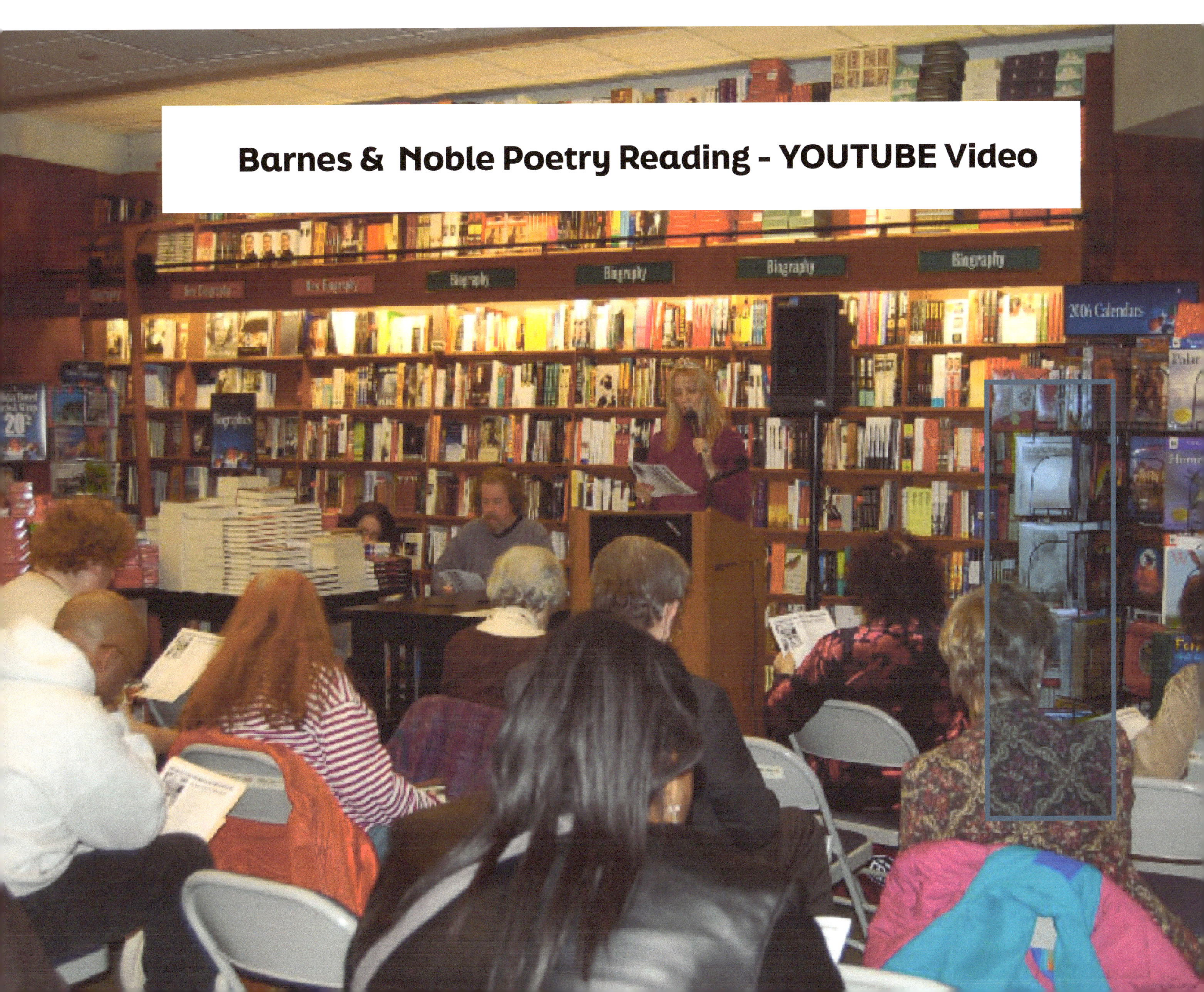

Barnes & Noble Poetry Reading – YOUTUBE Video
Biography
Biography
Biography
Biography
2006 Calendars

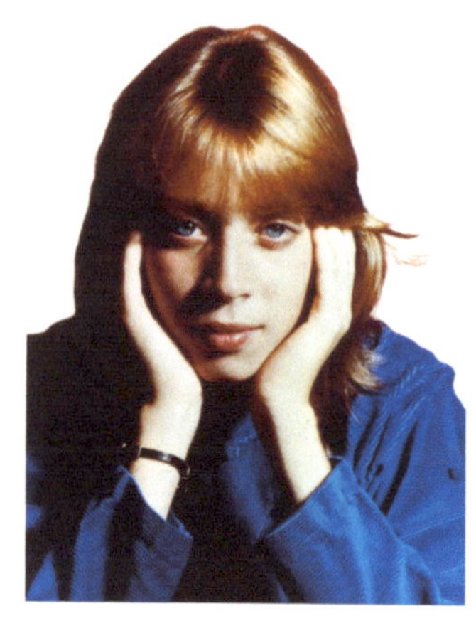

GENIUS: THE GIFT OF DIVINE REVELATION

MY BOOKS WRITE THEMSELVES

I Am Mortal
MY BOOKS ARE IMMORTAL
Please Handle My Books Gently
My Books Are My Remains

Part 1. Birth of Poem: 2008
Part 2. Poem Is Published in Poetry Books
Part 3. Format Book: January 2025
Part 4. Publish Book: February 2025

Sharon Esther Lampert
SEE THE WORLD THROUGH THE EYES OF A CREATIVE GENIUS
Prodigy, Prophet, Philosopher, Poet, Paladin of Education, Physicist, Psychobiologist, PINUP

FANS@SharonEstherLampert.com